If You Love Me Keep My Commandments

Lord Teach Me How

Candace Sims

Copyright © 2020 by Candace Sims

All rights reserved. No part of this publication may be reproduced by any means, graphics, electronic, or mechanical, including photocopying, recording, taping, or by any information storage retrieval system without the written permission of the publisher except in the case of brief quotations embodied in critical articles and reviews.

Candace Sims/Beacon Talent Development

PO BOX 18712

Atlanta GA 31126

www.beacontalentdev.org.

Author website: www.concepts-power.com

Unless otherwise indicated, scripture is taken from the Zondervan King James Version.

If You Love Me Keep My Commandments/ Candace Sims

ISBN-13: 978-0-9992815-3-6

Library of Congress Control Number: 2020912870

Dedication

This book is dedicated to my son Marcus D Reid (DOD 4/8/2007) and the many Marcus D Reids across the nation.

ACKNOWLEDGEMENTS..................................ix

INTRODUCTION:...1

                              The Ten Commandments: What's The Fuss?.............4

CHAPTER 1:   The First Commandment.................6

CHAPTER 2:   The Second Commandment...............13

CHAPTER 3:   The Third Commandment...............19

CHAPTER 4:   The Fourth Commandment...............25

CHAPTER 5:   The Fifth Commandment...............31

CHAPTER 6:   The Sixth Commandment...............38

CHAPTER 7:	The Seventh Commandment...............44
CHAPTER 8:	The Eighth Commandment...............50
CHAPTER 9:	The Nineth Commandment...............56
CHAPTER 10:	The Tenth Commandment...............62
CONCLUSION:	The Ten Commandments: What's The Fuss?...........68

ABOUT THE AUTHOR....................................71

Acknowledgements

Everyone has a story to tell. The challenge is telling it. I've always wanted to write a book, but I never considered myself a good writer. That has been the primary reason why I don't write. Upon completing this book, I discovered that it's not about writing at all; it's about telling a story.

The Ten Commandments were taught to me as a child. In my household, they were the basic principles of doing good and instructions for loving right. In the mind of a young child, the

Ten Commandments are not hard to grasp; you simply memorize them, recite them on Sunday morning, then go about your way continuing to play.

The hidden message in the Ten Commandments is they are actual instructions to peace and harmony for daily living. What once began as simple lessons to impress our parents and ministry leaders, are now {realized} undisputed truths that evolve to keep life simple, keep us out of trouble, and give us the way out of tangled circumstances. The beauty in the Ten Commandments is they have never changed. The Ten Commandments are and have been constant.

As I wrote, I thought about what each Commandment meant to me. I penned it to reflect a personal conviction that draws me closer to the One who desires to share everything with me. My desire is that as you read each Commandment, it deepens your love, honor, and respect for your Creator. A strong contentment with who you are will be revealed. My prayer is that it will give you a brighter perspective on connecting with principles meant to keep us in harmony with one another.

I truly believe God did not create us just to drop us off into a world of chaos, to leave us there struggling to figure out how to come up out of it. He loves us! The magnitude of His Majesty is reflective of His love for us displayed in the works of His hands. This is my response to how the Ten Commandments speak to me.

Introduction

The family unit is the primary example of amazing relationships. Everything is to be taught in the home. Some homes do a better job of teaching and instruction than others. Growing up, I had a mother, father, five blood brothers, and three blood sisters. One brother and one sister were through my father with a different mother, but I (even at 52) still adore them as if we shared the same mother. I will add, two of my sisters often communicate with my father's ex-wife just the same. This is because of a "root" of love from the heart that runs deep. There was not much envy, jealously, hatred, or discord among us siblings because we were taught to love each other. As we grew older, we discovered a higher calling to love God, higher than we did one another. This made the love we have for each other grow deeper each day.

Working as a Community Advocate, I often encounter crime victims adamant about their rights being denied, and the need for creating new laws. When I explain the purpose of original laws, it has the effect of cutting the heart like a double-edged sword, because it cuts going in and cuts coming out. It always brings responsibility back home to the source.

God's commandments are not intellectually confusing. What they are, is difficult to abide by for the self-indulgent nature. They help us to understand that specks in our neighbor's eye are logs in our own eyes. Logs so big that we are blinded by our own twisted and confused ideology.

The word "Command" can be quite intimidating. Do not be afraid of what God commands you to do. If you know and understand Him, you will find the harsh word (command) will lead you into a life of peace, courage, and confidence to live freely in any situation or circumstance.

My hope is that this little book, reintroducing the Ten Commandments, will help us straighten some crooked paths and lead us to more peaceful, serene circles of communication with those we know and consider as family members and those who are our neighbors but strangers.

God included everything. He summed it up in the Ten Commandments. You may find these Commandments erected in Courts of Law, yet barely referenced. Defense; it's now about what you can justify to defend your stance. The courtroom judge and the prosecutor listens. The jury of your peers weigh in, but it is ultimately the Heavenly Judge that will rule.

The Ten Commandments:

What's The Fuss?

MOTIVATED BY OBEDIENCE

We now understand that the Ten Commandments were God's original, absolute law and no other law will ever be needed to maintain and restore order in this world.

Dear God,

_____
_____
_____
_____
_____
_____
_____
_____
_____
_____
_____
_____
_____
_____
_____
_____
_____
_____

Date: _____

CHAPTER 1

The First Commandment

THOU SHALT HAVE NO OTHER GODS BEFORE ME.

This is the very first commandment from God. It is probably the first thing you were ever taught when you first studied the Bible; "there shall be no other gods before me." To have no other gods before Him is not selfish because you will see that once you love Him, He shares the deepest intimacies about Himself with you. The first thing we learn about God is His nature; how it is impossible for Him to not love you? Before He created humanity, He created the heavens and the earth and everything in it. All that He created was beautiful. With all this beauty surrounding us, He had to create human beings to enjoy it. But, before He created humanity, He rested. When He created you, He had to step back and say to Himself, "It is good; all good."

This first command is so important because not only does it create a foundational love in our hearts towards God, it helps us to love others as we love ourselves. Once you get this understanding, then and only then, are you able to love yourself. When God created humanity in all of its' uniqueness and differences, He said, "it is good." He (God) made the choice and determination that you, beloved, are good as you are. From the texture of your hair, or the lack of, to the tips of your toe nails, every inch of your creation is good, acceptable, enjoyable, worthy and codified in His love of you. What He thinks of you matters.

It is important to grasp a spiritual view of how God sees you and go about your daily tasks in that "truth."

Jesus calls us to love our neighbor as we love ourselves. The truth in this command is that the things you hate the most about other people are the very things you hate most about yourself. You tend to see them clearly in others. If you are not able to love yourself, you can't possibly love others. God's plan was not designed that way. He doesn't want us to love others more than we love ourselves. There is another abnormal extreme; to love yourself so much that you love no other. Love has balance. Love is plentiful. When you feel your love has left you depleted, you are to go straight to the source for a refill.

God has even defined love in the First Book of Corinthians in the thirteenth Chapter. He shares with us what love is and what love is not. I had to let go of my selfish and superficial definition of love because it was serving me and my family and friends no purpose. I was loving people the way I wanted to love them, from a heart that lacked true love. That is why my relationships always felt wrong, unsatisfying, empty, and short lived. It's easy to say, "I love you" in the heat of the moment (to get what you want); then hate the person you were with and the very space and time you lent to them. If I had loved God the way He defined love, I would have saved myself from a lot of shame and misery from all the failed relationships of my lifetime. I would have had the ability to understand what true love is and would not have settled for less. There would have been less forgiveness needed- first from God, then for myself, then for others-without expecting forgiveness in return.

God loved us long before we even knew who He was or what He was about. He is our wellspring of life and love. It's a spring of never-ending, abundant supply of care and concern. When we are empty, we go to Him to fill our cup, not things. He is the bank from which we can make daily withdrawals without any interest. To not have love in your heart is your choice, not God's. He doesn't even give us a reason why He loves us so much; teaching us that we need no reason to love one another. We love because He first loved us. Jesus didn't come to abolish the original law; He came to show us how to embrace the law.

The First Commandment:

Thou Shalt Have No Other gods Before Me.

MOTIVATED BY OBEDIENCE

The first Commandment is set to teach you to love God with all of your heart, mind, soul, and strength. This takes daily practice. Take a few days to make Father God your only God; be strong in your love for Him.

Dear God,
_____
_____
_____
_____
_____
_____
_____
_____
_____
_____
_____
_____
_____
_____
_____

Date: _____

CHAPTER 2

The Second Commandment

THOU SHALT NOT MAKE UNTO THEE ANY GRAVEN IMAGE, OR LIKENESS OF ANYTHING THAT IS IN HEAVEN ABOVE, OR THAT IS IN THE EARTH BENEATH, OR THAT IS IN THE WATER UNDER THE EARTH.

Idols are all around us. They become our obsession. We can't eat, sleep, or think until we feel at one with "our idol." It's stupid to have idols.

Once we come to know and love God, then we give Him His proper place in our lives. Idols can come in many forms or fashions, but I think the biggest idol one can have is "food." Yep, that's right- food! God knows we need it. We can go without it for a few days, but after about three days we are back at the table enjoying our fill. Greed is not the only way to determine how much we idolize food, but our choices of food can be seen as idolatry. God has provided all the delicious and nutritious foods on the planet good enough to sustain a healthy mind and body. But, no - we want what we want; the sweets, the breads, the butters, the crunch, the salty, and by gosh- the MEATS!

Did you know that in order to be set apart as God's holy people, we have to pay attention to what we eat? There are foods that are delectable yet make us lethargic and lazy. Foods that give us a burst of energy, then wear off and we're slouching around again. There are foods that just make us go "uuuuum and ooooh it's so good," with our eyes rolling around in the back of our head! But how can you effectively do God's work if you don't have the energy and clarity to be worthy of the task at hand?

Food obsession is at an all time high. If we make it to 45, or 50 years of age, our food choices catch up with us by way of aches, pains, inches, and pounds, packed on that are nearly impossible to lose. Diseases like hypertension, high cholesterol, diabetes, and a host of other ailments are not what God intended for us when He created us.

Whole foods were intended to satisfy the human craving and keep us healthy, vibrant, glowing, and strong. There is nothing processed about whole foods. We can even grow some of them ourselves.

I won't spend too much time talking about other idols like cars, entertainers, homes, money, fame, wealth, etc. I feel the strongest truth in idolatry is food. Daniel shows us by giving us his example. Or, the story about quails and manna is another lesson that teaches us about food choice and gratitude. Don't forget Eve, Esau, and Samson! The distance in understanding greed and idolatry from head to heart can be a matter of 40 days or 40 years. It is sad that a man will train for a whole year to eat the most hot dogs, at a hot dog eating contest, for money and a dusty trophy; rather than train for a year to incorporate delicious and nutritious foods to nurture the body towards strength, vitality, and wellness.

But God, through His love, has so much patience for us. His image is enough. If we pray to Him daily, immerse ourselves in His Word, and if we desire to draw nearer to the One who satisfies, then all is needed is Him. It is foolish to replace our Heavenly Father with someone or something else. Our Father God in heaven never disappoints. Try not to rely on symbols and objects of worship to remind you to hold the Heavenly Father in His rightful place in your heart. Draw nearer to the One who holds a place in His heart for you.

The Second Commandment:

Thou shalt not make unto thee any graven image, or likeness of antyhing that is in heaven above, or that is in the earth beneath, or that is in the water under the earth.

MOTIVATED BY OBEDIENCE

The first four Commandments teach us about God's love. This Commandment warns us to never replace God's image with anything. We begin to pattern our reliance on Him only.

Dear God,

_____
_____
_____
_____
_____
_____
_____
_____
_____
_____
_____
_____
_____
_____
_____
_____
_____

Date: _____

CHAPTER 3

The Third Commandment:

THOU SHALL NOT TAKE THE NAME OF THE LORD IN VAIN.

"Oh My God!" "Jesus Christ!" "Holy Mother of Jesus!" "God damn it!" "Son of a Bit—"; I think you get the point. We've all said it at some point in our lives. It's a vain expression of disgust or over emphasized excitement that's short lived. If this has become a pattern, you must learn to increase your vocabulary. There are hundreds and thousands of words in the English vocabulary to use for thoughts of expression. God's name is Holy, and He expected holiness from His people. This vain usage of His name came about from the wicked behavior of His people. The Jews were so sinful as His Holy chosen people. They started profaning the name of God! God created our brains with the ability to solve one problem one hundred different ways. I'm certain we can find better words of expression to identify what we are feeling at any given moment.

Let your "yes" be "yes"; and let your "no" be "no;" any further explanation proves that your reputation isn't trustworthy. Integrity and honesty will carry you far in life. When you are truthful all the time, you are credited as trustworthy. Tell the truth all the time.

Gossipy- don't you just hate when all people want to do is gossip? People gossip to shift the focus off of themselves towards other people. It's called "self-avoidance." They know their problems are so deep, evil, wretched, and wicked, that they don't want any part of the communication to be focused on themselves. That used to be me. I remember my mother on the phone with "The Price Is Right" blaring in the background, talking to her girlfriends, gossiping. I knew it was wrong, yet I grew up doing the same thing to other people. I thought everyone did it. I was so insecure and had so many hidden sins and secrets that I would bring up other people's stuff first, to divert the focus from me. I became so repulsive to be around that I found the loneliness gut-wrenching. A gossip betrays trust. No one will ever want to include you in their circle. Thank you, God, that I repented from this detestable sin.

"...and Oh Father God, I pray for my mother... and Oh Father God, help me to do well on this interview...and Oh Father God...and Oh Father God..." Have you ever been in a prayer circle with someone who prays this way? Do you find it hard to connect and focus on what the prayer need is, through all the "Oh Father Gods?" God tells us how to pray; Jesus shows us how to pray. Prayer should be like an honest conversation that flows. When you talk with your friend Sheila or Mike, you don't repeat, "...and Sheila, I was so disgusted with my boss that...", "...and Sheila, I went to the

Mall and got those shoes!" "...But Mike, I need to go cut my grass...but Mike, I need some gas in my mower...and Mike, I wish I could borrow $5...and Mike, I'll return it tomorrow!" Sounds absurd doesn't it! When you pray to God, He wants you to give Him enough of your attention-especially in a circle prayer- that it's like it's just you and Him.

All of these examples describe some ways of misusing God's name. Mishandling the hallowed name of God and its reputation can only be changed once you admit that it is wrong and out of place for God's people. It's a simple mind shift that you may have to practice over and over again before you get it. With God's help, you can begin to converse with Him so fluidly and smoothly that all you'll always want to talk with Him. You will rise to be the person that people always want around! You'll be a great speaker and an honest friend. Remember, Hallowed is His name.

The Third Commandment:

Thou shall not take the name of the Lord in vain.

MOTIVATED BY OBEDIENCE

Omitting undesirable words from your vocabulary is proof of true repentance. We can show love and dislike accordingly without cursing and being profane. Ask God to give you a new song. Be kind.

Dear God,

_____
_____
_____
_____
_____
_____
_____
_____
_____
_____
_____
_____
_____
_____
_____
_____
_____
_____

Date: _____

CHAPTER 4

The Fourth Commandment:

REMEMBER THE SABBATH DAY AND KEEP IT HOLY.

Have you ever said, "It's just not enough hours in a day." I still do! That's my cue that I'm doing way too much. God commands us to take one of His Holy days and dedicate it back to Him. In my honest opinion not because He needs it, but because WE need to! No one works harder than God.

In the very beginning when He put His hands, breath, and mind to work to create a universe of brilliancy, He worked for six days straight. Then He rested. I don't even think He was tired; I just think He wanted to relax and enjoy the masterpiece of His work! It was so beautiful that it took a whole day to behold its' beauty; the blue waters; the different shades of greenery; the multitude of flowers all different colors and scents; the curves-grooves-and-dips of the mountains and valleys! The smell of nature! The strong tall trees! The fluffy, pillowy clouds! I have not even begun to describe the fruits and vegetables and animals He created! Lo' What a Glorious Sight for mere mortals to behold! God wants us to feel what He feels when He embraces His Glorious works! He wants us to see, smell and taste what His intentions were when He designed all things! If we could, it would take an entire day to enjoy!

Taste and see that the Lord is good! Taste with your eyes! Smell with your eyes! Satisfy your hunger for more knowledge of God on your Sabbath Day! God requires a tenth of everything we have. That is called a tithe. Anything over a tenth is called an "offering." To tithe and to give an offering is the practice of sacrifice. Offering our bodies to God is our worthy sacrifice. We lose out on nothing when we give to God. Look at what He has created already! He even created us last because He wanted to share what He created with us.

Once we make up in our minds that the seventh day will be our Sabbath Day that we set aside for God, everything else will align and all that we do will be effortless. Sacrifice requires that we relinquish something that we value and cherish. We give it up for others to enjoy. We now enjoy watching others enjoy the things we once had. On your Sabbath Day, get up and get yourself ready for your worship service. God will be there already awaiting your gifts-gifts of service, gifts of caring, gifts and offerings --giving your heart in true worhsip. Give Him your all! Once your service in your house of worship is complete, then go home and open the Word with your family (or just you, if you are single) and study, read, and learn His ways. Get yourself some needful rest. Make sure you cook enough the day before so you won't have to spend an hour cooking. Drink nothing but water to flush your system.

Fill your mind and heart with Gospel/Christian music. People usually come out of their Sabbath at dusk. I usually take this time to prepare for the next day or the entire week. I feel myself already going into a new week calmer, fresh and well rested.

Who, other than God, knows what we need? He rested from His work-all of His work. He rested enough to create something more splendid and marvelous than everything else He created...Us! He saved the best for last. It is not much to give Him the first (not last) of what we have. Like Cain and Abel, the measure of your sacrifice to God is measured by what you have already decided in your heart to give.

The Fourth Commandment:

Remember the Sabbath Day and keep it Holy.

MOTIVATED BY OBEDIENCE

When is enough, enough? Let God show you that He can meet that unmet need, so that you can give what's required to Him. The Sabbath set aside for Him. It is actually needed for us.

Dear God,

_____
_____
_____
_____
_____
_____
_____
_____
_____
_____
_____
_____
_____
_____
_____

Date: _____

CHAPTER 5

The Fifth Commandment:

HONOR THY FATHER AND THY MOTHER.

To me, this is one of the hardest commandments to obey. I feel this way because I, like most people, have a sinful nature of self-indulgence. "It's all about me." "Gotta look out for number one because if I don't, who else will?" Well, if we are properly taught, we know that God looks out for "numero uno;" so that you can carry on your business of loving Him and others. I hope you are seeing the pattern here. Once you grasp the depth and magnitude of the first four commandments, everything else falls in line.

I know what you are thinking, so let me just get right down to the point. I felt like I didn't have parents worthy of honor either. I have my story and I'm sure you have yours. I am about to squash any preconceived notion you have that has been justifying your reasoning for not giving honor to your "absent" parents.

When Jesus, as a boy, (in the context of Him not doing away with the commandments but rather fulfilling them) was in Jerusalem with His earthly parents, celebrating the Passover, they unknowingly left without Him, to head back home. They were already a days' journey away when they realized He was not with them! Now, how about that for abandonment! They didn't realize their son wasn't with them until they were a day's journey into their travels. When they got back to Jerusalem, I'm sure they were frantically/ anxiously looking for Him. When they found Him, He was in His Father's house. Let's stop here- Jesus was honoring the first commandment; the one He was taught as a young boy-by those imperfect parents. He wasn't lost. He wasn't left alone because He was there teaching what He knew about The Father. He wasn't scared or kidnapped; He was in his Father's house. As an earthly parent, I couldn't even be mad. If I were them, I'm sure they were thinking about sharing some of the responsibility for not being aware that He wasn't with them.

Jesus loved God the Father, and demonstrated it by honoring his earthly parents. How do we know? It is because He went home with them. Later, in adulthood, when He hung on the cross, He asked for His mother to be cared for.

This could have been the worst case of child neglect, but instead it was the most gracious form of mercy; a shining example to follow to honor His parents because of the love of God. You may not have had the best set of parents coming up; however, you can change the trajectory of your generational line by simply following God's original rule.

I wanted my son to honor me as much as my parents wished that I would honor them. Teach your children to honor their parents; but parents, know that there is a responsibility unto God from you as well. Honor your parents all your life, for long life. The roles of caregiving may change. To be the teacher for generations to come, you must be the honorable example. If your parents are dead, honor them in death. Children of the next generation will have no clue where they are going if they are not taught to honor and respect the elders. It matters to know from where you come, but it is better to know how to get where you are going-the elders know. There is no new formula for parenting.

Let's just follow the original rule. Here is what it looks like: don't make fun of your parents, do not put your parents down by shaming them. If your parents are difficult to deal with and be around, set boundaries for yourself and ask God for the strength of patience and self-control. If your parents have a different set of values from God's original law, then politely respect their opinion and gently state your stance. Do not argue and do not debate with your parents. You might not like it. It might not be pleasant at the current time. But in the end, you'll experience a long, serene life with no regrets if you honor your parents.

The Fifth Commandment:

Honor thy father and thy mother.

MOTIVATED BY OBEDIENCE

Everyone has a reason why they justify defying this command. No reason is acceptable. You honor your parents and leave the rest up to God. He sees your mistreatment. His justice is fair and timely.

Dear God,

_____
_____
_____
_____
_____
_____
_____
_____
_____
_____
_____
_____
_____
_____
_____
_____
_____

Date: _____

CHAPTER 6

The Sixth Commandment:

THOU SHALL NOT KILL.

Killing destroys. Satan comes to steal, kill, and then all is destroyed. For those who are not delivered from unspiritual patterns of thought, death will destroy you. If you hold the Word of the Lord close to your heart, and if death shall appear to a family member, you will grieve, but you will recover. Jesus died once for all. His death brought new life to this temporary temple that will constantly need repentance and deliverance until our own death comes.

Death affects more than just the person who falls to death. The pain can extend out to immediate family members, church members, coworkers, community associates, and more. To maliciously kill another human being is one of the cruelest acts anyone can do. It's fatal; there's no undoing it. It's hard for some to forgive and unforgiveness interferes with love- the greatest Command. There are situations where death comes about accidentally and unwilfully. These latter examples have spiritual and mental consequences far less relenting then malicious intent.

When Jesus warns us by commanding us to deal with the raging anger in our hearts, what He is really doing is helping us so that those thoughts won't manifest into murder. When I was 15 years old, I made a decision to get an abortion out of fear, shame and embarrassment. I had slept with a boy, not fully understanding that intercourse without protection would make me a mother way before I was ready. He was the first boy I had ever slept with. I was so ashamed that I didn't even want to tell my mother. But the instinct mothers have, showed that she knew I was pregnant even before I admitted it. My mother pleaded with me to not abort the baby. With tears and prayer, my mother expected me to change my mind. My mother, a black woman, birthed all seven of her children. Four were by a white man, in the deep south- South Carolina- in the late 1950s. Her pleas were not enough to convince me to change my mind and I aborted my baby. It wasn't until 11 years later, at the age of 26, I confessed this sin before my baptism. I believe that God has forgiven me. However, not a day goes by that I don't wonder what the sex of that baby was, who it might have looked like, or what kind of talents it would have possessed. I have these thoughts more so, as I have lost a child, to murder in 2007, at the age of 22. The repercussions I face daily are my consequences to an act of self-indulgence for my own benefit. The thoughts never go away, and daily, as I love the Lord, it keeps me from succumbing to the guilt.

God values life; if He didn't, He would not have allowed Christ to die for the entire world. No one is singled out to be loved by God. His love is inclusive. You first need to understand how much He loves you. Once you do, your entire life changes. If I had understood how much God loved me at 15 years old, I would not have been seeking love from Emmanuel. Yes, that is actually the name of the boy whom I've gotten pregnant with. In it, He has a sense of humor; I did not even know the name Emmanuel means "God with us." Boy, if we only knew spiritually that God was with us-I mean really knew- this outcome would have been different; better. God would have helped us rear the baby.

The Omnipotent nature of the Heavenly Father is with us from birth till death. Every day, whispering instruction and tenderly offering His love to shelter and keep us from harmful decision making. He can take away our intent to cause harm to others and ourselves.

The Sixth Commandment:

Thou shall not kill.

MOTIVATED BY OBEDIENCE

Murder or the intent to kill should be far from the thoughts of a heart of one who loves and is loved by God. He is our source. And if death comes, He is the one who brings comfort.

Dear God,

_____
_____
_____
_____
_____
_____
_____
_____
_____
_____
_____
_____
_____
_____
_____
_____
_____

Date: _____

CHAPTER 7

The Seventh Commandment:

THOU SHALL NOT COMMIT ADULTERY.

When God created Adam, He said, "it is 'real' good." I, as a woman, get it; when I see a man and observe his masculine physic, I have often said, "He is fine!" However, Adam realized he was lonely. All of the animals had a mating partner; he had none. God knew what Adam was thinking and went to work. God put Adam in a deep sleep, took one of his ribs and created the perfect image for him- for any man- "a woman." You think the physique of a man is a killer, just look at the shapely stature of a woman. Now, I am all woman-meaning I am attracted to the opposite sex-but when I see a female with banging natural curves more distinct than mine, sometimes I can't help but to look at what God had created in her! God designed men to be visual; and women too. It's natural to look. Temptation starts with the eyes and is not limited to the physical body (food for example).

The attraction between male and female is dynamic! It is indescribable! It's magnificent! It's alluring! It's natural. Natural. Natural. (Once more) Natural. So, let's get spiritual about the subject. Our natural desire to long for something is innate within us. Our natural nature is to desire it even more if it belongs to someone else. There is power in the taking of things that are not originally ours. It's conquering. But it is also destructive, damaging, and can sometimes be fatal. We are called to die to our human nature daily.

Adultery has to do with sex. If no sex is involved in male/female relationships, than it would not be considered adultery. Just being together can raise the suspicion of "a hint" that there is more than a friendship. There are many passages that warn us as humans to deal with our unnatural desires for sex. They include sex with self, sex with animals, sex with the same sex, sex with objects, sex while single, and sex with someone who is pledged in marriage to someone else. The issue here that calls forth our attention is "sex." When you come into a sexual union with another, you become joined with them; attached and almost affixed to them. You create yourself such a web of bondage that you begin to crave their actual presence- all the time! This longing then transcends to an entitlement which moves towards ownership. The greatest gift you can give your spouse is your purity; it's a gift that never gets old.

Adultery is deep. This is how deep it is: the church is the 'bride,' and Christ is the 'bridegroom.' There is nothing Christ would not do for the church. He died for the church. He claims the church as His own. We were bought at a price (not a cheap price).

When two people are joined together in marriage, they leave the home of their parents and cleave to one another and form a tighter union. Nothing should interfere to disconnect this union from strengthening. A strong marriage breeds secure children. A strong marriage adds value to flourishing communities. A strong marriage encourages a stable economy. In a strong marriage, you will find trust, dependability, refuge, and a foundation that sets a perfect example for generations to come on how to structure families.

When God created man, it was good. When He created woman, man said that she was really good! God's design for marriage between a man and a woman is as good as it gets! He creates somebody for everybody. We are to wait on the product He has designed for us. We might get it right sometimes; but He gets it right all the time. When we allow Him to reward us with that unique desire, every day will be a blessing, even the bad days. She's there to compliment him; he's there to compliment her; together, they complete one another. Let no man draw your marriage asunder.

The Seventh Commandment:
Thou shall not commit adultery

MOTIVATED BY OBEDIENCE

If this is not your personal truth, it's time to reshape your assessment. Separation still means married. It is wrong before the eyes of God to take another person's spouse for your own pleasure.

Dear God,
_____
_____
_____
_____
_____
_____
_____
_____
_____
_____
_____
_____
_____
_____
_____
_____
_____

Date: _____

CHAPTER 8

The Eighth Commandment:

THOU SHALL NOT STEAL.

Where did we go wrong to think that stealing something will bring a win? I'm thinking of baseball. When a runner steals a base and makes it to third base, then eventually is driven in to step on home base for the run, someone still loses. Musical chairs- when the music stops and a chair is taken-one person is left standing. I even grew up hearing the saying, "I'll beat you like you 'stole' something." That indicates that this beating will be brutal! The heart of a man who has to win by cheating and stealing reveals there is a root evil that needs to be dealt with; Pride. God did not create us in His image to have ill intent.

Picture a five-year-old; the scene is four pieces of candy left in a dish on the table. You step away, leaving the child in the room. You come back into the room and there are only three pieces of candy left. You ask, "Where did my piece of candy go?" The response, "I don't know." You ask, "Did you eat my candy?" The response, "No." You, the parent, know that you didn't eat the candy. You know the child not only stole, but the vulnerability led to a lie.

The devil is deemed the father of lies; hence he is the father of liars. When you lie, the truth isn't in you. We are God's children. We are not to lie; we are not to steal or cheat. It is unrighteous and unrighteousness should not be celebrated. Stealing comes as a package deal; you also have to lie. Those who steal don't want to be known as a thief, so, they lie. Once you've told so many lies, you become unrecognizable and untrustworthy. You lose yourself. You lose sight of who God is and what He represents.

The antidote to stealing is gratitude and servitude. Stealing can get you killed, which we discussed in a previous chapter. No one expects to have their property invaded by an intruder. The startling encounter can produce fatal results. The solution: ask, seek, and knock. God says you don't have because you don't ask. He didn't intend for you to "take" what you don't have. Why is it hard for us to ask for what we want? It has to do with vulnerability. We do not want to hear, "No, you cannot have that." Eve stole from God when she ate from the tree. Adam stole from it too, because she gave some to him. They were told not to touch the fruit from this specific tree because it belonged to God. Wisdom and knowledge were what they obtained, but in obtaining these characteristics, they realized they were naked. They were ashamed and vulnerability set in. God knew that in our humanity, we are not comfortable with facing the things that make us vulnerable/naked. I believe it was His intention for Him to deal with vulnerability alone, to leave all the details to Him.

The wisest of us won't quite have all the answers that vulnerability asks. Vulnerability is a cousin of insecurity. Before they ate the fruit they stole, they didn't know they were naked. The wisdom they came into exposed the trouble they were in, and they tried to hide from the one who knew what they had been told not to do. Scripture says in Genesis 2:25 (before they ate), the man and his wife were naked. They were not embarrassed, nor were they afraid. They didn't have the wisdom to know they were naked until they ate the stolen fruit. God asked, "Who told you, you were naked?"

The five-year-old responded, "I didn't eat the watermelon candy," The parent responded, "How do you know the flavor was watermelon?" Yes, stealing may bring us into a revelation of something interesting, but it does not erase the fact that you stole in order to come into this new knowledge. Do not steal; just ask.

The Eighth Commandment:

Thou shall not steal.

MOTIVATED BY OBEDIENCE

God help us to take the sin of stealing serious. It's not petty; for stealing reveals more about our hearts that we are willing to admit.

If You Love Me You Will Keep My Commandments   55

Dear God,

_____
_____
_____
_____
_____
_____
_____
_____
_____
_____
_____
_____
_____
_____
_____
_____
_____
_____
_____

Date: _____

CHAPTER 9

The Ninth Commandment:

THOU SHALL NOT BEAR
FALSE WITNESS.

A false witness is a liar. A witness is a truth bearer. A false witness will never be trusted. What's worse is when you lie for financial gain. When someone says, "I'll need you to stretch the truth," they have run out of justifications to prove their stance. No one shows up to lose. Every runner steps up to the start line intending to win. "I need you to throw this game/fight because I need this win, and I'll share the earnings with you. Don't worry about what people will say. It'll die down in a few days; however, you'll be paid. In a year, they will love you again." God Bless the American Way!

As God's children, we put God's reputation on the line when we bear false witness. The image of God becomes distorted when we claim to live in Him, yet we lie. We make it hard for people to become willful, truthful, and faithful followers of God through false prophecy. Bearing false witness against your neighbor shows that you do not love him. Hence you do not think enough of yourself and your reputation. Most importantly, you do not show that you love God. Bearing false witness brings us full circle back to understanding our need to love God with all of our strength. It takes strength to back down from a tempting, lucrative evil, especially if you are in debt. We justify our actions because we needed the money. God said, "Just ask," remember? But then it's that vulnerability that He knew we were unwilling to admit.

One of the most deplorable lies is when a preacher will claim to have healed an unassuming disabled person. There had to be a conversation beforehand and an agreed amount of compensation between the two. The preacher has increased his notoriety and increased his pockets.

Another reason why we bear false witness against our neighbor is because we don't even know them. Vulnerability stops some from getting to know a person. We size them up by society's standards and begin spreading untruths about them that in the end makes us look stupid. The power of life and death is in the tongue. This unsuspecting neighbor is symbolic of the many men who sat in defense court of their fate, just to have a liar swear to false witness about false truths of the case. The fate of this person's life is driven by a lie just to bring the case to an end, with little regard to the life of the innocent person accused. Adequate investigation brought no win for the prosecution, so they resorted to a false witness. This not only destroys the defendants' life, his family, the defense attorney, but more so it tarnishes the justice system. An

African proverb says, "When two elephants fight it is the grass that suffers." Nothing can grow in stained lifeless soil. Justice is blind because justice is for all. One person can't win for the land to heal; we all have to work together. Escaping punishment isn't a win.

If I can't get what I want, then it might not be for me to have. God is trying to win back your heart. You will wear yourself ragged, running with the same empty scheme, day to day with a razor-sharp tongue. Although the scales of justice seem unbalanced, God, with His ten thousand, will prevail over the man with twenty thousand. God doesn't need a lot to spring forth His purpose. He just needs truth and honesty from you. Let your yes be 'yes.' Let your no be 'no.' His plan is always at work and unfolding right before our eyes. Just as grass grows effortlessly- not by our constant watching- it grows. Will you be a false witness or a faithful witness? The choice is yours.

The Ninth Commandment:

Thou shall not bear false witness.

MOTIVATED BY OBEDIENCE

Grasping God's view makes life simple. Be a faithful witness rather than a false one. It will go well with your conscious. Life is summed up by how you value people and your relationships.

Dear God,

_____
_____
_____
_____
_____
_____
_____
_____
_____
_____
_____
_____
_____
_____
_____
_____
_____
_____

Date: _____

CHAPTER 10

The Tenth Commandment:

THOU SHALL NOT COVET.

"What you see is what you get" ain't always what's best for us. I've come to know that when trouble persists, it isn't what's around you that causes the grief and trauma, but rather what's in you. The eyes are the window to the soul; it's good to close them sometimes! When we close our eyes, we are able to shut out the cravings and desires of the world that creates the chaos and confusion in our mind. Close your eyes for a moment and just allow your eye lids to rest atop of the cheek bone...ahhhh, that feels so good.

When we covet the things that do not belong to us, we begin to set our course on a path of destructive practices that make life more harder than it ought to be. When we covet the things that are not in the will of God for our lives, all we do is prolong the inherent blessing that is already ours to receive. It took the children of Israel 40 years to travel through the desert to the promised land (unfocused), when it should have taken two weeks! For most of us, all it takes is a simple "mind-shift" to get back on track. God intended for us to bask in the joys, gifts, and talents of others, rather than wanting them to be our own as well. The longer you focus and covet what others have, the longer it takes for you to discover your own unique gifts. If you have a heart that finds it hard to celebrate the wins of others, then you have some work to do to get your heart right.

It starts with the eyes, then the thoughts develop in the mind. It is wrong to want the wife/

husband of your neighbor. God specifically commands against this. However, it is also wrong to covet the clothes, jewels, the shoes, the speaking ability, the texture of hair, and anything else you may not have that belongs to someone else. Be yourself! Enhance what you have! Don't cause gifted people to dumb-down their gifts and talents just to make you feel comfortable (vulnerability/insecurity). Laws of attraction work when we are grateful; grateful first for what we have (and sometimes grateful for what we have not)! That's why it is so important to have a Gratitude List. I'll be the first to admit that sometimes it's hard to sit down and begin the process of being grateful for ALL I have. At times ALL you see is debt, or all you have is pain. Pain hurts. Until we are taught to understand that pain leads to passion, we will avoid the lessons that pain teaches us. God said, "Let the only debt you have be a debt of love." The distance of a shift change from head to heart can be a "minute" or a "mile." The choice is yours. God gives us a head start by warning us to not covet anything of our neighbors that isn't ours.

In an earlier chapter, we talked about "do not steal; just ask." Once we come to know and understand all that God commands us, we will begin to see how they all intertwine and work together for our good, to make us whole before the one who knows us best. I am imploring you to ask God to help you deal with your heart. Stop justifying destructive habits and behaviors by saying, "Oh, God knows my heart." Yes, He does; it's now time for you to start dealing with the unbecoming patterns of disparaging actions and thoughts that leave you lost, alone, depleted, and broke. Use the Ten Commandments as a starting point.

God gives us everything we need for life and godliness. If we do not have it yet, it could be on our path awaiting for us to arrive to it. You may have to go through difficult times to reach the desired result. It's character building. Covetous behavior- taking what doesn't belong to you, and not utilizing your own gifts and talents-is character damaging. Your reputation in on the line on how you listen to and abide by God's Commandments. Fix your eyes on Jesus, and your heart, soul, mind, and strength will follow.

The Tenth Commandment:

Thou shall not covet.

MOTIVATED BY OBEDIENCE

We now understand that the Ten Commandments were God's original, absolute law and no other law will ever be needed to maintain and restore order in this world.

If You Love Me You Will Keep My Commandments

Dear God,

_____
_____
_____
_____
_____
_____
_____
_____
_____
_____
_____
_____
_____
_____
_____
_____

Date: _____

CONCLUSION

The Ten Commandments: What's The Fuss?

No matter where you are at this point in life, it's never too late to turn to God to reverse the patterns that keep you wandering lost in deserted places. The book of Ecclesiastes helps us to understand what's meaningful and meaningless, both at the same time, in real time. We must have balance. Christ is the balancing scale that weighs our thoughts and attitudes. What He thinks matters. The Pharisees knew it; they wouldn't admit that what Jesus thought mattered. Jesus is the Master Teacher.

Jesus is the Master Advocate. His care and compassion are second to none. He teaches us to forgive, to show mercy, to cancel/write off debts, and tell the truth-the whole truth; and nothing but the truth. He gives us the right to remain silent, and the courage to snitch. He is our Private and Public Defender. He judges justly. As our Heavenly Judge, He laid down the laws of the land that are not politically motivated or tipped to favor the rich. His laws judge the thoughts and attitudes of every heart. As the Master Advocate, He is fair. Life isn't fair; some of us die at birth, some of us die before we reach our 20s, and some of us live to be 103 years old. Life just isn't fair, but Jesus is.

We were bought at a price; some of us make Him work hard for the cost that was paid. Over, and over we keep making the same mistakes. Some hear it one time and it clicks! He is so patient; He wants everyone saved! His patience teaches us to be patient with others in order to celebrate once one comes into the realization of the truth.

If you are new to the teachings of the Ten Commandments, let them be a sweet, sweet satisfaction to the confusion in your life. If you've heard of them since your childhood, take the time to embrace and etch them on your heart as your personal promise to break the bad patterns in your life. At 52 years of age and new to Victim Advocacy, I've turned back to the laws I learned as a youth to help those who otherwise would see no means to an end. After losing my only living child to a senseless murder that has gone cold, the only advocacy that keeps me faithful is the advice from the Master Advocate. My Advocacy is built on the foundation of Jesus' Advocacy. There is no other way.

About The Author

Candace Sims is a Victim Advocate, Bereavement Coach, and Program Director for Advocacy Support. Originally from Buffalo, NY, she moved to Atlanta, GA in 1988 and has resided there since. The loss of her son Marcus D Reid at the age of 22 years in 2007 was the beginning of her journey towards Community Advocacy and Bereavement.

As an effective Community Advocate, one must know and understand victimization as it is, and the feelings and emotions it evokes. While learning how to navigate within the Criminal Justice System as a Victim Advocate, she understands how the system is designed to administer justice fairly; however, people in positions of enforcing, teaching, and administering justice are flawed. We can't change people, but how we carry ourselves as victims and survivors can change the way people of position view us. Facts care nothing for feelings and vice versa. There is a place to learn the facts, and a place to express your feelings for holistic healing.

Candace never had an assigned Advocate to help hold her hand through her traumatic experience. She never expects another parent to have to wonder about "What to do next?" Her Advocacy is all about taking responsibility for your role in your journey to steer your ship in a forward-moving direction, especially if no earthly justice is rendered.

You can find peace in pain; you can live in honor of your loved one. God shows us the way through His way.

Index

A

abandonment, 32
adultery, 44, 46, 48
advocacy, 70, 72

B
balance, 8, 69
blessing, 47, 63
bridegroom, 46

C

celebrate, 63, 70

chaos, 63
children, 34, 40, 47, 51, 57, 63
church, 46
command, 3, 8, 36, 64
compensation, 58
confusion, 63, 70
courage, 3, 69
covet, 62–64, 66

D

death, 34, 38–39, 41–42, 58
deliverance, 39
distance, 15, 64

E

earth, 7, 13, 17
embarrassment, 39
energy, 14
entertainers, 15

F

forgive, 39, 69
forgiveness, 9

fruits, 26, 52–53

G

generations, 34, 47
gifts, 27, 46, 63–65
gossip, 20–21
gratitude, 15, 52

H

heaven, 7, 13, 16–17
honesty, 20, 59
honor, 32–36, 72
honoring, 33
humanity, 7, 52

I

idolatry, 14–15
idols, 13–15
instructions, 1
intentions, 26, 52
intercourse, 39

J

Jesus, 8, 10, 19, 21, 32–33, 38–39, 65, 69
journey, 32, 71–72

K

knowledge, 26, 52–53

L

laws, 2–4, 10, 66, 69–70
lessons, 15, 64
liars, 51, 56, 58
Lord, 19, 23, 26, 38, 40

M

marriage, 46–47
mercy, 33, 69
mistreatment, 36
money, 15–16, 57
murder, 39–40, 42

N

neighbors, 3, 8, 57–58, 64

O

objects, 16, 46
offerings, 26–27

P

pain, 15, 39, 64, 72
patience, 16, 34, 70
patient, 70
peace, 3, 72
power, 45, 58
pray, 16, 21–22
prayer, 21, 40
preacher, 58
price, 46, 70

R

realization, 70
repentance, 23, 39

S

sacrifice, 27–28

scripture, 53
service, 27
sex, 40, 46
shame, 9, 39
shoes, 22, 64
sin, 40, 54
sleep, 13, 45
soul, 11, 62, 65
steal, 38, 50–51, 53–54
stealing, 50–54
strength, 11, 16, 34, 57, 65

T

Temptation, 45
tithe, 26
tongue, 58
truth, 8, 15, 20, 51, 56, 59, 69–70

U

unforgiveness, 39
union, 47
unrighteous, 51

V